UNDERDOGS

SPORTS CHAMPIONS

★
★
★

SUPER SOX
BREAK THE CURSE

★

★
★

BY MARTIN GITLIN

45th PARALLEL PRESS

Published in the United States of America by Cherry Lake Publishing Group
Ann Arbor, Michigan
www.cherrylakepublishing.com

Reading Adviser: Beth Walker Gambro, MS, Ed., Reading Consultant, Yorkville, IL
Series Adviser: Virginia Loh-Hagan
Book Designer: Jen Wahi

Photo Credits: cover: REUTERS/Alamy Stock Photo; page 5: © Toasterb at the English language Wikipedia project, CC BY-SA 3.0, via Wikimedia Commons; page 7: © Jerry Coli/Dreamstime.com; page 9: © Frances P. Burke, Public domain, via Wikimedia Commons; page 13: © Jerry Coli/Dreamstime.com; page 15: © Keith Allison, CC BY-SA 2.0, via Wikimedia Commons; page 19: © Jerry Coli/Dreamstime.com; page 23: © Jerry Coli/Dreamstime.com ; page 25: © Dreammediapeel/Dreamstime.com; page 29: © AP Photo/Sue Ogrocki, File

45th Parallel Press is an imprint of Cherry Lake Publishing Group.

Library of Congress Cataloging-in-Publication Data

Names: Gitlin, Martin, author.
Title: Super Sox break the curse / written by Martin Gitlin.
Description: Ann Arbor, Michigan : 45th Parallel Press, 2023. | Series: Underdogs. Sports champions | Audience: Grades 4-6 | Summary: "Super Sox Break the Curse takes readers inside the famous 2004 Boston Red Sox-New York Yankees American League Championship game leading up to the Red Sox 2004 World Series win. Provides background leading up to the game, review of the game, why the world was shocked, and what happened afterward. From players no one believed in to teams no one thought could win, Underdogs: Sports Champions covers some of history's greatest underdogs. Written in a strong narrative nonfiction style, the storytelling in these books will captivate readers. The series includes considerate vocabulary, engaging content, clear text and formatting, and compelling photos. Educational sidebars include extra fun facts and information"-- Provided by publisher.
Identifiers: LCCN 2023005883 | ISBN 9781668927762 (hardcover) | ISBN 9781668928813 (paperback) | ISBN 9781668930281 (ebook) | ISBN 9781668931769 (pdf)
Subjects: LCSH: Boston Red Sox (Baseball team)--History--Juvenile literature. | American League Championship Series (Baseball) (2004) | World Series (Baseball) (2004)--Juvenile literature.
Classification: LCC GV875.B62 G58 2023 | DDC 796.357/640974461--dc23/eng/20230216
LC record available at https://lccn.loc.gov/2023005883

Cherry Lake Publishing would like to acknowledge the work of the Partnership for 21st Century Learning, a network of Battelle for Kids. Please visit http://www.battelleforkids.org/networks/p21 for more information.

Note from publisher: Websites change regularly, and their future contents are outside of our control. Supervise children when conducting any recommended online searches for extended learning opportunities.

Printed in the United States of America
Corporate Graphics

TABLE OF CONTENTS

Introduction

What makes sports fun? Fans love watching sports. They love watching great athletes. They love seeing the best in action. They're awed by their skills. They're awed by their talent.

But what makes sports interesting? One never knows what will happen. Fans can expect an outcome. Their side could win. Or their side could lose. Nobody knows for sure.

Sometimes an upset happens. This is when a team that's expected to win loses. Upsets make fans sad. They confuse people.

Sometimes an underdog rises to the top. Underdogs can be players. They can be teams. They have little chance of winning. Yet, they win.

David Ortiz celebrates after hitting a home run.

Surprises happen. They're shocking. But they're wonderful. They're fun to watch.

That's why games are played. That's why fans watch games. They don't know who's going to win. They don't know who's going to lose. This is the point of sports. Not knowing is exciting.

Upsets in sports are legends. Legends are great stories. They're remembered forever. Underdogs make people smile. They inspire. They give hope. There are many sports champions. The most loved are underdogs. This series is about them.

Pedro Martínez, pitcher for the Boston Red Sox, pitches against the New York Yankees.

Warming Up

It was 1919. It was the day after Christmas. Christmas is a time of gifts. The people of Boston were gifted with Babe Ruth. Ruth was the best baseball player. He was called "The Great Bambino." Bambino means "baby." It's an Italian word. Ruth played for the Boston Red Sox.

Harry Frazee owned the Red Sox. He had a secret. He wanted to get rid of Ruth. And he did. He sold the slugger. A slugger hits a lot of home runs. Frazee sent him to the New York Yankees.

Red Sox fans were stunned. They were mad. They got madder when Ruth turned the Yankees into a dynasty. A dynasty is a ruling family. The Yankees won many games. They won the World Series. The World Series are final games. They're played to determine the champions.

Babe Ruth during his time on the Boston Red Sox. People say the Curse of the Bambino started when Ruth was sold to the New York Yankees.

The first team to win 4 games takes the title. The Yankees won titles year after year.

The "Curse of the Bambino" had begun. Red Sox fans thought they were cursed. They thought they were punished for trading Ruth. They were still being punished 86 years later. They lost the World Series in 1942. They lost in 1967. They lost again in 1986.

They were also tormented by the Yankees. Tormented in sports means often losing to the same team. The Yankees beat the Red Sox often.

In 1978, the teams had tied for the division title. A one-game playoff was held at Fenway Park. That was the home of the Red Sox. The Red Sox were ahead. Bucky Dent played for the Yankees. He was a weak hitter. He stepped up to bat. He blasted a home run. He won.

Red Sox fans got madder. The Yankees beat them in the playoffs. This happened in 1999. The Red Sox had another chance in 2003.

How unlikely was the blast that beat the Red Sox in 1978? Bucky Dent hit just 5 home runs that season. He had not hit one for 7 weeks. The 2003 homer by Aaron Boone was less surprising. Boone had started that season with the Cincinnati Reds. He hit 18 home runs for them. He was then traded to the Yankees. He mashed 6 more home runs. He played in the All-Star Game that year. It was the only time he earned a spot. The game features baseball's best players. One team has the best players from the American League. The other has the best from the National League. Both the Red Sox and Yankees play in the American League. They've been in that league since 1901. That's the year it started.

It came down to one game. The winner would go to the World Series. The Red Sox gained a 4–0 lead. Pedro Martínez was a Red Sox ace. Ace means the team's best pitcher. But Martínez began to tire. Grady Little was the manager. Managers run baseball teams. Little refused to remove him.

Red Sox fans shouted at their TV sets. They begged Little to replace Martínez. Little did not. The Yankees tied the game at 5–5. Aaron Boone played for the Yankees. He was another weak hitter. He stepped up to bat. He hit a home run. The Yankees won.

Most people don't believe in curses. But many Boston fans do. They believed in "the Curse of the Bambino." Was it real? Could they ever win against the Yankees? They would get their answer a year later.

Pedro Martínez winds up for a pitch. Many believe manager Grady Little refusing to take Martínez out of the game against the Yankees in 2003 ruined their chances of winning.

The Upset

The year was 2004. The date was October 16. The event was Game 3 of the playoffs. The site was Fenway Park. The Red Sox fans were in a bad mood.

The series was not over. It just felt that way. The Yankees were again beating the Red Sox. The Curse seemed alive and well. The Yankees scored 5 runs. They did this in the fourth inning. They added 4 more. This happened in the seventh inning. They gained 2 more. This happened in the ninth. (Baseball games are divided into 9 innings. An inning is a turn to bat.)

The Red Sox didn't just lose. They were clobbered. The final score was 19 to 8. Nearly everyone believed it was all over. The Yankees had won the first 3 games of the series. They only needed 1 more. They seemed destined for the World Series.

New York Yankees pitcher Mariano Rivera was known by many as the "best closer ever." He knew how to wrap a game up with a Yankees victory.

No team behind 3–0 in the playoffs ever won. That had never happened in baseball history.

The Red Sox fell behind. They fell behind 8–0 in the opening game. They lost 7–10. The Yankees led throughout Game 2 and Game 3. But then there was Game 4. Nobody expected what happened. The Red Sox won that game. People were surprised. Some thought the Red Sox had given up.

Game 4 didn't look good. The Yankees led 4–3. It was the ninth inning. The ninth is the last inning unless there's a tie. Three more outs and it would be over.

The Yankees' top pitcher was on the mound. That was Mariano Rivera. Many believe he was the best closer ever. That is the pitcher who tries to finish off victories.

The Red Sox seemed to be done. Fans felt "the Curse of the Bambino." They blamed Harry Frazee for trading Babe Ruth. Few thought they could win. The Yankees were too good. But the Red Sox believed in themselves. And that's all that mattered.

BEYOND SPORTS

★ Babe Ruth's real name was George Herman Ruth Jr. His father had the same name.

★ Ruth was a troubled youth. His parents struggled with him. They sent him to Catholic school. Ruth said, "Looking back on my boyhood, I honestly don't remember being aware of the difference between right and wrong."

★ Ruth appeared in 4 movies. He played himself. In 1942, he was in *The Pride of the Yankees*. He lost 40 pounds. He did this to play a younger version of himself.

★ There's a candy bar named Baby Ruth. The company said it's not named after Ruth. It claimed to name the candy after Ruth Cleveland. Ruth Cleveland was the daughter of U.S. President Grover Cleveland. But Cleveland died in 1904. The candy was created in 1921. Babe Ruth was a star at that time.

The Shocker

The 2004 Red Sox seemed doomed. They were down 3–0 in the series. They were losing 4–3 to the Yankees. It was Game 4. All eyes were on Mariano Rivera. Rivera needed 3 outs to end it. The Red Sox were all but done.

Then it happened. It was a glimmer of hope. Rivera let a batter reach first base. Then Dave Roberts also made it to first. Roberts was fast. He had guts. He took off to steal second base. He barely made it. But he was safe.

Red Sox fans cheered. Bill Mueller played for the Red Sox. He singled to tie the game. He hit the ball. He got to first base. The Red Sox were saved from defeat. But they hadn't won yet. David Ortiz was a slugger. He became a hero. He smashed a home run. The Red Sox won!

★ David Ortiz smashes a single against the Yankees!

Fans were happy. But the Red Sox still needed to win more. They needed to take 3 games in a row. That's the only way they'd get to the World Series.

The Yankees took a 4–2 lead. It was late in Game 5. The Red Sox were again doomed to lose. But they had what the Yankees didn't have. They had Ortiz.

Like Ruth, Ortiz had a nickname. He was known as "Big Papi." He came through again. He singled in the fourteenth inning. He clinched victory.

Now the Yankees were worried. It didn't matter. The Red Sox were on fire. They couldn't be stopped. They scored 4 runs early. They did this in Game 6. They held on. The series was tied. Game 7 was a blowout. Stunned Yankees fans watched. The Red Sox were ahead 6–0.

Then it was all over. The Red Sox won. The final score was 10–3. Players and fans rejoiced. They jumped for joy. They shouted. They hugged each other.

The Curse of the Bambino wasn't yet dead. The Red Sox needed to win the World Series. But the curse was dying. And beating the Yankees felt so sweet.

SAME SPORT, DIFFERENT STORY

The New York Mets had been a joke. They finished last or near to the last. They were bad from 1962 to 1968. But then, they began to win. They had great pitching. Tom Seaver was their ace. He was perhaps the best in baseball. The Mets were good in 1969. They won 41 of 50 games. They took first place. They beat the Chicago Cubs. They were called the Miracle Mets. First, they beat the Atlanta Braves. They did this in the playoffs. But could they beat the Baltimore Orioles in the World Series? Few people thought they could. The Orioles had won 109 games that year. That's one of the best baseball records ever. Yet the Mets didn't just win. They dominated. They lost the first game. Then they won 4 in a row. The 1969 Mets were the greatest underdog story in baseball history.

The Response

The Red Sox were thrilled to beat the Yankees. They felt a sense of revenge. This means they wanted to get even. They had gotten the Yankees back for the 1978 loss. But they still felt the sting from the 2003 defeat.

Yet it was not all about revenge. It was also about pride. They fell behind 3–0 and still won. They were the first team to do this. Terry Francona was the manager. He said, "We fought back. And we did it against a great, great team. What we did was really something. We're so proud of these guys."

One player made it possible. That was David Ortiz. His story is amazing. It's also similar to Babe Ruth's story. Ortiz was let go by the Minnesota Twins. This happened in 2002. They didn't think he was good enough. What a mistake! Ortiz was traded to the Red Sox. This happened in 2003.

★ David Ortiz points to the sky after slamming a home run.

Ortiz was a great leader. He was respected. When he talked, his team listened.

He was a super slugger from the start. But he was more than that. Ortiz was a clutch hitter. That means he came up with huge hits when needed most. That was certainly true in the defeat of the Yankees. He mashed the home run that won Game 4. He blasted one in Game 5. Then he hit the single that won it. Ortiz cranked another over the fence in Game 7. That came in the first inning. It put the Red Sox ahead to stay.

Ortiz inspired his teammates. He gave a pep talk. He did this after they lost their first 3 games. He told them that loyal Red Sox fans deserved better. His speech worked. He also turned his words into action. He did this by leading the Red Sox to victory.

Their work wasn't done. They needed to truly end the Curse. They could only do that winning the World Series. A very strong St. Louis Cardinals team awaited.

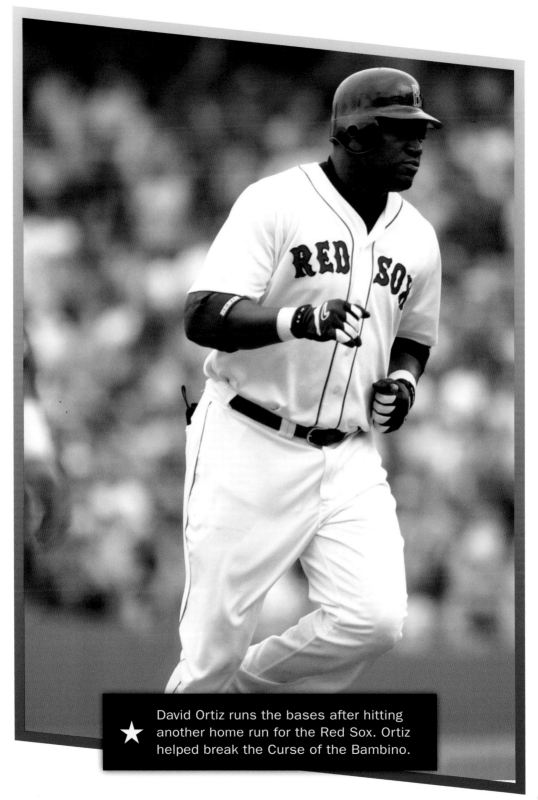

David Ortiz runs the bases after hitting another home run for the Red Sox. Ortiz helped break the Curse of the Bambino.

Moving On

It was late October 2004. There was something in the air. This World Series was going to be different.

That feeling was everywhere. It was felt by the Red Sox. It was felt by their fans. Beating the Yankees gave the Red Sox momentum. This is a feeling that can't be stopped. But the Cardinals promised a tough fight.

Boston fans packed Fenway Park. They watched both teams play. The Red Sox forged ahead 4–0. They stretched their lead to 7–2. The Cardinals tied it at 7–7. The Red Sox went up 9–7. The Cardinals tied it at 9–9. It was exciting.

Someone needed to step up. And it was Mark Bellhorn. Bellhorn played for the Red Sox. He was a hitter. He was just an average player. But he sent a ball soaring. The ball bounced off the foul pole in right field. It was a home run!

Keith Foulke (29), Doug Mientkiewicz (13), and catcher Jason Varitek of the Red Sox celebrate following their 2004 World Series win.

The Red Sox held on. They won. Fans were thrilled. Their team was like a machine. No foe could slow them down.

Even the pitchers came through. Curt Schilling played for the Red Sox. He was a pitcher. He shut down the Cardinals in Game 2. The game moved to St. Louis. Now Cardinal fans could root for their team. But it didn't matter. The Red Sox were on a roll.

Pedro Martínez allowed no runs in Game 3. Manny Ramirez hit a home run. The Red Sox pushed ahead. Soon the Sox were celebrating another win. They needed just 1 more. Then they would be king of baseball. They wasted no time in Game 4. Johnny Damon played for the Red Sox. He was the first batter. He smashed a home run. That was all the pitcher needed. Derek Lowe was the Red Sox pitcher. He shut out the Cardinals. It was over. The Red Sox had won their first title since 1918.

Fans went crazy. The city hosted a parade. It was quite a party. More than 3 million people attended. They came from all over the world. Fans had suffered for so long. But their team had finally killed the Curse. They clinched it against the Cardinals. The amazing upset of the Yankees made it possible.

★ ★ ★

Curt Schilling was a Red Sox pitcher. He was inspiring. He pitched Game 6 against the Yankees. He had an ankle injury. His ankle was bleeding through his sock. Yet he still beat the Yankees. He joined the Red Sox in 2004. Few expected greatness. He was 37 years old. He was older than most. He had been pitching in the major leagues since 1988. He was a super pitcher. He shocked the world. His best season was with the Red Sox. He won 21 games. That led the American League. He finished second in the Cy Young Award voting. That honor is given to the best pitcher every year. Schilling was still going strong at age 40. That's when he helped Boston win another title. He won another World Series game in 2007. The Red Sox beat Colorado that year.

Learn More

Books

Gitlin, Marty. *Baseball Underdog Stories*. Edina, MN: ABDO Publishing, 2018.

MacKinnon, Adam C. *Baseball for Kids: A Young Fan's Guide to the History of the Game*. Berkeley, CA: Rockridge Press, 2020.

Savage, Jeff. *David Ortiz*. Minneapolis, MN: Lerner Classroom, 2015.

Tavares, Matt. Growing Up Pedro: *How the Martinez Brothers Made It from the Dominican Republic All the Way to the Major Leagues*. Somerville, MA: Candlewick Books, 2017.

Explore These Online Sources with an Adult:

Britannica Kids: Baseball

Kid Nation: Boston Red Sox

Sports Illustrated Kids (Baseball)

Glossary

ace (AYS) The best pitcher on a team

closer (KLOH-zer) A pitcher who tries to close out victories

clutch hitter (KLUCH HIH-ter) Someone who can get a make big hits when the team needs it most

dynasty (DIE-nuh-stee) A long period of often winning titles

inning (IH-ning) 1 of 9 parts of a baseball game during which both teams get to bat

legend (LEH-juhnd) An extremely famous story that is told many times

manager (MAN-uh-jer) A person in charge of the players on a team

momentum (moh-MEN-tuhm) The feeling of teams or players that all will continue to go their way

revenge (rih-VENJ) The feeling of getting even

singled (SIN-guhld) Hit a ball and made it to first base

slugger (SLUH-ger) A great player who hits a lot of home runs

tormented (TOR-men-tid) In sports, to lose over and over again to the same team

underdog (UHN-der-dawg) A player or team that has little chance of winning but ends up winning

upset (UHP-set) When the team that is expected to win loses

World Series (WURLD SEE-reez) Annual baseball series that decides an overall champion team

Index

About the Author

Martin Gitlin is a sports book author based in Cleveland. He won more than 45 awards as a newspaper sportswriter from 1991 to 2002. He won a first-place award from the Associated Press in 1995 for his coverage of the World Series. Marty has had more than 200 books published since 2006. Most were written for students.